First published 1991 by
M.J.M. Publications, Sissinghurst Court,
Sissinghurst, Kent TN17 2JA

ISBN 0 9518631 0 X

Designed by John Clement
Typeset by Mainline Typesetters,
St. Leonards-on-Sea, East Sussex
Printed and bound in Great Britain

HORRIBLY RUDE!
THE BOOK THEY BANNED IN BASILDON!
FILTH!
DISGUSTING!
THE OFFICIAL
ESSEX GIRL
JOKE BOOK
Compiled by
BEVERLEY MILLER
Illustrated by
JEFFY GORILLA
You've seen the knickers..
now read the book!

How do you make an Essex girl laugh in the middle of the night?

Tell her a joke at breakfast time.

How do you drown an
Essex girl?

Put a mirror on the bottom of the swimming pool.

What does an Essex girl use for protection during sex?

A bus shelter.

What is an Essex girl's mating call?

"Ooh! I feel really drunk".

Why is an Essex girl like a carpet tile?

After she gets laid she gets trodden on.

What do you say to an Essex girl
who can suck a golf ball
through a garden hose?

Marry me!

What did the cabbie say to the Essex girl when she dropped her knickers in lieu of the fare?

"Haven't you got anything smaller?".

What does an Essex girl do to relieve stress?

Changes hands.

What’s the difference between an Essex girl and a dose of the clap?

You can get rid of a dose of the clap.

What is the difference between an Essex girl and a supermarket trolley?

A supermarket trolley has a mind of its own.

What is the difference between an Essex girl and the Titanic?

Only 1,490 men went down on the Titanic.

Why does an Essex girl wear knickers?

To keep her ankles warm.

Why is an Essex girl like an old washing machine?

They both leak once they're f****d.

How does an Essex girl turn off
the light after sex?

She slams the door of
the Cortina.

How do you make an Essex girl's eyes light up?

Shine a torch in her ear.

What is the difference between an Essex girl and the Dartford tunnel?

The Dartford tunnel has a
toll booth.

What is the difference between an Essex girl and a bus?

A bus has to come before you
jump on it.

What is the difference between an Essex girl and a Rubik's cube?

You need both hands and more than five minutes to do a Rubik's cube.

What is the similarity between an Essex girl hitchhiking and a Lada?

They're both f****d after five minutes on the road.

What do you call an Essex girl who screws ten men a day?

An under achiever.

Why did the Essex girl take her Rotweiler to a party?

The hostess told her to bring her own liquor.

Why can't an Essex girl get a bloke to eat ice cream out of her fanny?

No-one can eat that much
ice cream.

What did the Essex girl say when she discovered her diamonds weren't for real?

I've been raped!

Why does an Essex girl slide down the bannister before sex?

To warm up dinner.

How many Essex girls does it take to screw in a lightbulb?

None. Essex girls only screw
in Cortinas.

What do you call a Surrey girl
between two Essex girls?

An interpreter.

What's the similarity between an Essex girl and a dog turd?

The older they are the easier they are to pick up.

What does an Essex girl have printed in her knickers?

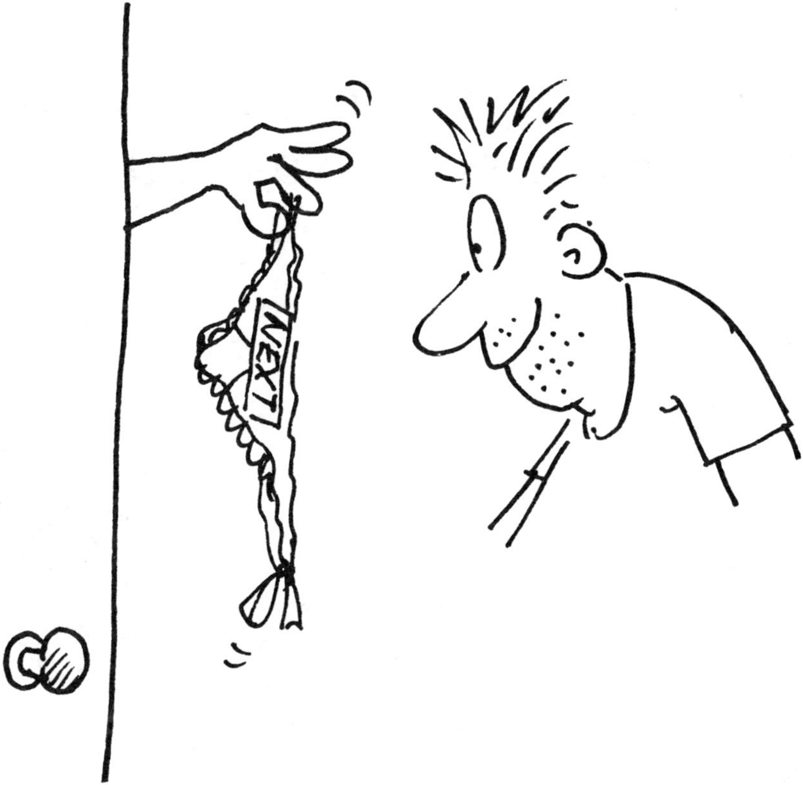

Next.

What is the difference between
an Essex girl and a walrus?

One is a fat, smelly thing with a
moustache and the other is a
sea mammal.

How can you tell if an Essex girl has been using a word processor?

Tippex marks all over
the screen.

What is the difference between an Essex girl and a computer?

You only have to
punch information into a
computer once.

Why does an Essex girl always give head after sex?

She likes to have her cock and eat it.

How can you tell when an Essex girl has an orgasm?

She eats her cigarette and
lights up her chip.

What's the difference between an Essex girl and an ironing board?

It is difficult to get an ironing board's legs apart.

What's the difference between an Essex girl and a washing machine?

A washing machine doesn't follow you around for a week after you used it.

What is the difference between an Essex girl and an Essex boy?

An Essex girl has a higher sperm count.

What happens to an Essex girl's asshole after sex?

He gets sent out for a
take away.

What is the difference between a pub and an Essex girl's clitoris?

An Essex boy can find the pub.

What does an Essex girl put behind her ears to make her more attractive?

Her feet.

What is the difference between an Essex girl and a meat pie?

A meat pie doesn't squeak
when you eat it.

What has an IQ of 150?

Essex.

What do you call 100 Essex girls floating together on the sea?

Isle of Dogs.

What is the similarity between an Essex girl's legs and the Beatles?

They haven't been together
since the 70s.

What is the similarity between an Essex girl and Gorbachev?

They both got f****d by seven men when they were on holiday.

What is the difference between an Essex girl and Gorbachev?

Gorbachev knew their names.

What is the difference between an Essex girl and a pit bull terrier?

Lip gloss.

What is the similarity between an Essex girl's boyfriend and a panda?

He eats shoots and leaves.

What is the difference between an Essex blonde and a plane crash?

Her black box is easier to find.

Why doesn't an Essex girl use the pill?

Because it keeps falling out.

What is the difference between an Essex girl and a Kit Kat?

You only get 4 fingers in a
Kit Kat.

Why does an Essex girl wear white shoes?

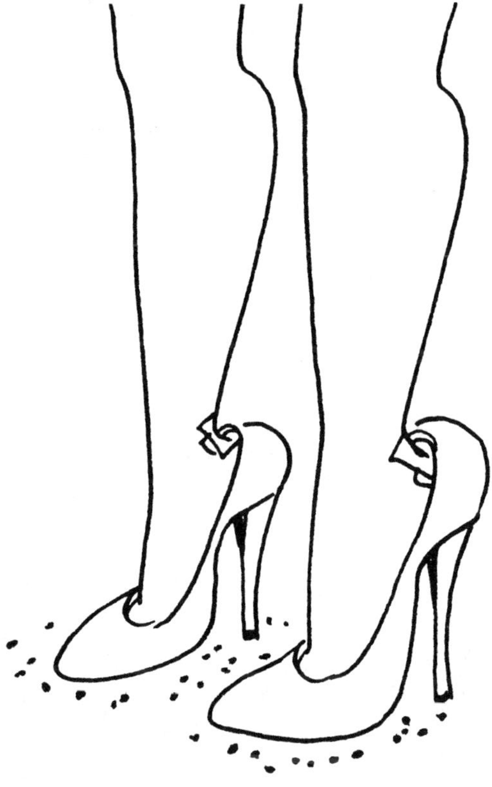

So the dandruff doesn't show
when she's got no knickers on.

Why does an Essex girl have C&A written on her knickers?

So she doesn't get them on
back to front.

What is the similarity between an Essex girl and a London tour bus when it's raining?

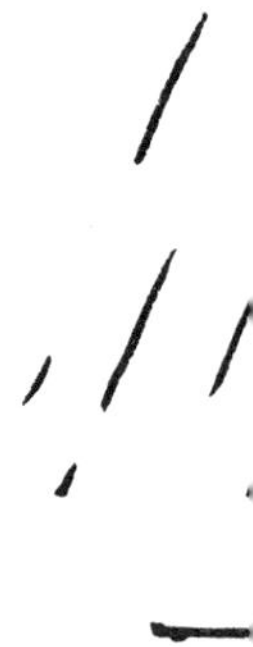

It's empty upstairs, but full up down below.

What's the difference between an Essex girl and British Rail?

You can sometimes get through to British Rail.

Why does an Essex girl douche with fluoride?

She heard it reduces cavities.

Why don't Essex girls wear knickers when they are speeding up the M11?

Because they like to be picked
up by the fuzz.

What is the difference between an Essex girl and a gorilla?

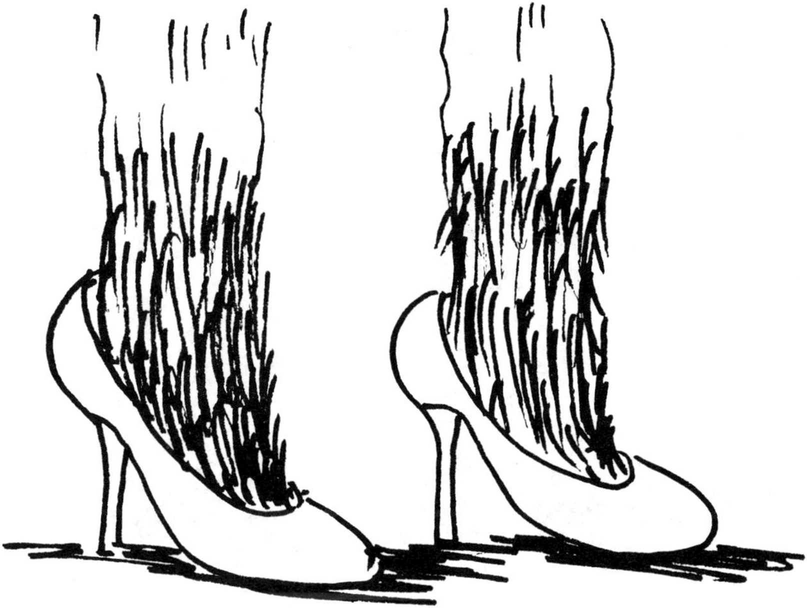

White stilletoes.

What does an Essex girl say after sex?

Do you really all play for the same team?

What’s the difference between a pregnant Essex girl and a lightbulb?

You can unscrew a lightbulb.

What do you call an Essex girl
with an IQ of 65?

A genius.